D1433444

PET OWNER'S GUIDE TO
TRAINING THE FAMILY DOG

Brian McGovern

RINGPRESS

ABOUT THE AUTHOR

Brian McGovern has been involved with Competitive Obedience for some thirty years as a highly successful handler, an instructor, and as a qualified Obedience judge. His training seminars have a large and enthusiastic following on both sides of the Atlantic. Brian has his own training school in Holland, and members have achieved remarkable success, winning over 400 first prizes in Obedience competitions. Brian, himself, has won the Dutch National Obedience Championship on two occasions.

The McGovern family dogs.

PHOTOGRAPHY

Photographs have been contributed by: Brian McGovern, Amanda Bulbeck, Carol Ann Johnson, Marc Henrie, Keith Allison and Steve Nash.

Published by Ringpress Books Limited,
PO Box 8, Lydney, Gloucestershire,
GL15 6YD, United Kingdom.

First published 1998
©1998 Ringpress Books Limited. All rights reserved

ISBN 1 86054 092 9

Printed in Hong Kong through Printworks Int. Ltd.

CONTENTS

5 OBEDIENCE EXCERCISES 49

Lead walking; The recall; Stationary commands; The sit; The wait; The down; The stay.

6 PROBLEM DOGS 62

Barking; Aggression (Dominant aggression; Predatory aggression; Fear aggression); Destructiveness.

7 HAVING FUN WITH YOUR DOG 72

Competitive obedience; Agility; Flyball; Working trials; Field trials; Just having fun.

Dog Owning: Fact And Fiction

Imagine wandering across a lush green meadow carpeted with many-coloured flowers, watching the children running ahead and playing with the family dog, a handsome Golden Retriever. You are secure in the knowledge that the children have a playmate, guardian and friend. Or perhaps you picture yourself strolling along the riverside on a warm summer evening, needing only the company of your magnificent, black-and-gold German Shepherd, to share the glorious sunset.

We all have a mental picture of what it would be like to have our very own dog. Some of my most precious moments have been shared with our dogs, walking along the beach early on summer mornings, before the heat of the

Owning a dog can be deeply rewarding – but you must also be prepared to care for your pet when the going gets tough.

day brings the tourists. Such times are indeed cherished moments of pure pleasure, and it is thoughts of these that encourage many people to buy a dog.

REALITY

However, there is another side to the coin. Imagine sitting in front of a warm log fire on a stormy, winter evening deciding whether or not to have a nightcap before slipping between the covers of a cosy bed. Then, just as you decide that one more drink would be a perfect end to an ideal evening, your spouse utters the dreaded words, "It's your turn to take the dog out".

Alternatively, you arrive home after inviting friends back for coffee after a night out. You look forward to the welcome you know you will get from Simon, your beautiful Irish Setter. As you open the door you expect to see him waiting for you, wagging his whole body as always, in typical Setter fashion. The first thing that greets you is not Simon, but an insidious odour that seems to have permeated the whole house. Dreading the worst, you look around to discover that dear Simon has had another of his bowel upsets, which only seem to

happen when he is left alone, has access to the sitting-room, and you have guests. Simon jumps up to say hello, placing two large paws on your chest, leaving two large, brown, paw prints on your best suit. Apologising profusely, the guests make excuses about baby-sitters and rush off, hoping to get to the end of the path before having to take another breath. Then, to finish off an exquisite evening, you hear the words you fear most "You can clean it up, it's your dog". Such is the life of a dog owner.

It is a sad, and regrettable, fact that the average family spends

Hopefully a dog will be part of your life for more than a decade, so give plenty of thought to making the right choice.

Size and temperament are essential factors to consider when selecting a breed.

more time and effort deciding which car, or new piece of furniture, to buy than in making the choice of which breed of dog to have, or if, in fact, they should have a dog at all. The average car is only kept for two or three years, whereas the average dog will probably be part of your life for more than ten years. The only person to suffer if you choose the wrong car is yourself, the owner. However, the moment you become a dog owner, you take responsibility for the welfare and care of a living creature who has the awareness and perceptiveness of a child. It feels pain, loneliness, fear, boredom, sadness, and all the other emotions normally only associated with humans. The training and responsibility of owning a dog is comparable to teaching and caring for a three-year-old child, but whereas the three-year-old child will mature, a dog will remain a 'child' throughout his life.

CHOOSING A BREED

In general, if you decide to have a pedigree dog, you will, with a certain degree of accuracy, be able to determine its size and appearance as an adult dog. A common misunderstanding is that the same can be said of a dog's character. "A Golden Retriever is a gentle dog that loves people", or "a German Shepherd is a guard dog and bites people", are the sort of comments I hear all too frequently. I have seen Golden Retrievers that could show the worst Pit Bull Terrier a thing or two, and I know of German Shepherds that have made excellent guide dogs, and are the most gentle of creatures. Most dogs, if they are typical of the breed, will probably show certain character traits of that breed. It would be fair to say that gundogs, and other breeds that have been

specially bred to chase or hunt game, will probably chase rabbits more readily than a Pekinese or a Chihuahua. This does not mean that all hunting breeds will have to be kept on the lead while in the country, or that all toy breeds will never poach the odd rabbit or two. It simply indicates that a certain character trait may be bred into the dog, and that this should be taken into consideration when making a choice of breed.

NURTURE AND NATURE

When choosing a particular breed it is worth noting that, within the breed, there are also enormous variations in character. It is therefore advisable to see both parents, and as many offspring, or other dogs from that bloodline, as possible. A character is formed by both inherited traits and environment. So, a good trainer can make an excellent pet of a dog with a bad character, and a bad owner can ruin a potential working champion.

By seeing several dogs of the same bloodline, you can get a more accurate picture of the inherent character traits which will indicate how your dog could be as an adult. At the risk of upsetting the canine world, I do not advise people to go to shows and ask the breeder for their opinion of the breed. I am not questioning the honesty of breeders, but I believe that they cannot always give an impartial opinion. In my experience, the best place to ask for information on your choice of breed is at the local dog training club, where the instructors are in constant contact with the different characteristics of various breeds, and can therefore can give an informed view through personal experience.

Most dogs are chosen for their looks, either out of a dog book full of pretty pictures, or because television has made them popular. Once the dog is in the house, it will be his character that will determine his relationship with the family. A Miniature Poodle in a large family full of teenage rugby players would probably be less suitable than a Labrador or a Golden Retriever. However, that same Poodle would fit perfectly into the life of a quiet, less active person. At the end of the day, it is a matter of personal choice. As long as you are willing to accept the responsibility of owning the dog, and understand the limitations of your chosen breed, then all that remains is to make sure that he is sound in body and limb before taking him home. The rest will be up to you.

CHOOSING THE RIGHT DOG

The choice of dog to buy can be extremely difficult. Large or small, pure-bred or cross-breed, puppy or adult? All these decisions have to be made before actually going out to find the dog of your choice.

The advantage of buying a pure-bred dog is that you will know approximately what the dog will look like as an adult. You should also have a reasonable idea of his inherent character. This cannot be said of a mongrel of unknown parentage, or of a cross-breed, where the parents are of different breeds. Some of the best dogs I have ever known have been mongrels, and it has been said that non-pedigree dogs are stronger, and more resistant to illness, than their pure-bred counterparts. Some pure-bred dogs cross well (Border Collie x Golden Retriever is a prime example), as the good points of both breeds seem to be passed on to the pups. However, I advise against German Shepherd crosses, of any type, as they often tend to be very dominant.

PUPPY OR ADULT?

If you decide to buy an adult dog, you will have the advantage of 'getting what you see'. The dog will, most probably, have attained his full growth, and his character will have been formed. You will not have all the problems associated with rearing a puppy, such as house training, and he may be partially obedience-trained. If you buy from an animal shelter you may be allowed to have the dog for a trial period, or perhaps you already know the dog. However, you should be wary of buying an adult dog from a complete stranger, because, as often as not, dogs are resold when they have caused the previous owner problems. This may also be true of a dog bought from an animal shelter. However, with a dog from a shelter, you should receive an impartial opinion from experts.

If you decide on a puppy, you should realise that rearing a youngster is extremely time-consuming, certainly comparable to having a baby in the house. The puppy's character is unformed – he has yet to learn any bad habits – so how the puppy turns out will be in your hands. The pleasures of owning a puppy are tremendous.

Puppies are fun to rear, but if you opt for an adult you will know what you are getting.

WHICH BREED?

Assuming you have settled upon a pure-bred dog, the next step is to choose a breed to suit you. World-wide there are more than 300 different breeds of dog. The Kennel Club in the United Kingdom has divided all recognised breeds into groups: Hounds, Gundogs, Terriers, Utility, Toys and Working, which is to be divided giving Pastoral as an additional group. In most other countries these same breeds are split into ten groups.

WORKING

Historically, this group contained almost all the shepherding breeds, such as the Collies, but these have now been placed in the new Pastoral Group. Some of the giant breeds, such as the St Bernard, are included in this group, and it also contains the Rottweiler. This is a breed that has become increasingly popular and, unfortunately, the breed has suffered as a result. When owned and trained by a responsible, experienced handler, this is a most rewarding breed, but the Rottweiler has a strong guarding instinct which can become dangerous if misdirected. It is definitely not a breed for the novice dog owner.

The Irish Wolfhound: A gentle giant, but too big for most households.

HOUNDS

Most of the Hound group are very old breeds, which were selectively bred for hunting. The Hound group includes dogs of all sizes, from the Irish Wolfhound to the Miniature Dachshund, and some breeds within this group can make excellent pets. However, there are others that do not readily adapt to being an obedient family dog, as they tend to be too independent.

Without doubt, the most popular breed of the Hound group is the Dachshund, of which there are six different varieties, in varying sizes and types of coat. The breed originated in Germany, where it was developed for hunting badgers. I find they make excellent house pets, are very easily trained, and although faithful

The Rottweiler: This breed needs an experienced owner.

companions, they can be very protective of their owners.

The Irish Wolfhound is another breed within the Hound group. This dog is a true gentle giant, and although I love the character, the size makes him unsuitable as a house pet for the average home.

GUNDOGS

As suggested by the name this group of dogs was bred to assist the huntsman when shooting game. The Gundog group can be sub-divided into three: the Pointers who are used, as the name implies, to point to the

The Golden Retriever: Steady and reliable, the Golden is one of the most popular companion dogs.

hidden game; the Setters and Spaniels, whose job is to flush the game out of hiding; and last but not least, the Retrievers, who were bred to pick up the shot game and return with it to the hunter. These dogs have the inherent instinct to use their noses to find game, and care should be taken with young dogs that they do not get the opportunity to develop this trait if they are to be kept as house pets.

Two extremely popular breeds of dog in the Gundog group are the Golden Retriever and the Labrador Retriever. At one time, the Golden Retriever was probably the house pet par excellence, and the better examples of the breed are still an ideal choice. However, as so often happens, the popularity of the breed can lead to its downfall, and I have seen many Golden Retrievers that were extremely vicious and dangerous. This problem is caused mainly by breeding for the show ring, without devoting enough attention to character. The Golden Retriever is also one of the world's most popular breeds for training as guide dogs, which is living proof of its friendliness, trainability, and reliability.

TERRIERS

The Terrier group was selectively bred to hunt game that would 'go to ground', or seek shelter from the huntsman by hiding underground. Originally, terriers had to be small enough to follow the prey underground, while, at the same time, strong and brave enough to fight and chase the game back to the surface. Many terrier breeds still have this inherent courage, which stems from the aggression needed to hunt.

The Jack Russell: A true character in the canine world.

The Jack Russell Terrier is one of the canine world's characters and, in the right hands, makes the ideal companion, as he is equally at home spending the day on your lap, or out in the fields. This is another dog that is very trainable; however I would not recommend buying a puppy from working parents as they can be a little on the sharp side, especially with regard to the local cats.

PASTORAL

This new group is an off-shoot of the Working Group, and includes the shepherding breeds.

One of the most maligned breeds of dog is the German Shepherd, or Alsatian, as he was once called. The German Shepherd has been used for almost all canine activities in the service of man. He is one of the most popular police dogs, while at the same time he is a proven guide dog. He is the first choice of the search and rescue services, and of the Military Police, as a guard dog. In the right hands, the German Shepherd Dog makes the most faithful and trustworthy of pets; however, he can be extremely strong-willed, and I do not advise a German Shepherd for the inexperienced owner.

The Border Collie: A workaholic that demands plenty of stimulation.

Another Pastoral breed that is becoming a popular house pet is the Border Collie. This breed is a true workaholic, so is an excellent choice for the active owner who intends to make a hobby of owning a dog. It is a very versatile breed and can adapt to almost any form of training.

Although they can make excellent pets, Border Collies are often too active and hyper to sit around the house all day, with an occasional walk around the park.

Anyone considering a Border Collie as a non-active house pet would be advised to look for an adult dog, so that you can see whether he is a quiet, non-neurotic type, before buying him. There are many quiet types about, but the average Border Collie needs to be kept occupied if you want to avoid problems.

TOYS

As the name implies, the Toy group contains the smaller breeds of dogs. To confuse matters, all small dogs are not necessarily part of the Toy group. These dogs were developed as human companions, and, as such, were probably the first dogs to be kept as house pets. Most of the breeds contained in this group make excellent companions. However, because of selective breeding to reduce size and alter the shape, many of the toy breeds have inherent physical deformities, which can cause health problems.

The smallest breed of dog in the world is the Chihuahua, with an average adult weighing in at about 2–3 kilos. Although small, the Chihuahua has a very large heart, and is often a bit standoffish with strangers, prepared to bark at anyone entering the room.

The Yorkshire Terrier: Lively and intelligent, this breed should not be underestimated.

Another small breed that is extremely popular is the Yorkshire Terrier. This very intelligent dog is the smallest of the terriers and should, in my opinion, be awarded his rightful place in the Terrier group. Although very small, he has all the characteristics typical of a terrier; lively, tireless, and feisty. He is often accused of being nervous because of his penchant for barking and yelping.

UTILITY

Personally, I have never understood exactly what the Utility group is, as it contains a mixed bag of breeds with no apparent logic behind their inclusion. A wise man once told me that all the breeds in this group are here because they did not fit anywhere else. Some of the more popular breeds in this group are the Poodle the Shih Tzu, and the Dalmatian.

The most popular dog in the Utility group is without doubt the Poodle, which comes in three sizes, Miniature, Toy, and Standard. The Standard Poodle was bred as a gundog and was extremely adept at retrieving water-game. The two smaller versions of the breed were bred from the Standard version. The Poodle is extremely popular as an Obedience Trials dog in America where it has enjoyed enormous success, perhaps proving that the European attitude that it is a nervous lapdog may be a little misplaced. In fact, the Poodle is extremely quick to learn, and very intelligent.

The most obvious advice is that you should not let your heart rule your head. But you probably will, we all do, so I will not bother to warn you against it.

The Standard Poodle: Poodles are bright and quick to learn.

2 *The New Arrival*

Once your preference of breed has been decided, and you have found a breeder with pups available, you have to decide whether you want a dog or a bitch. Many people shy away from bitches because of the inconvenience of their twice-yearly season. During this period, bitches are willing to mate, and therefore have to be watched. However, dogs are in heat the whole year round. Bitches tend to be less prone to arguments and fighting than dogs, but both dogs and bitches can make excellent pets, so the choice is really one of personal preference. I do advise all owners of pet dogs who will not be used for breeding to have them neutered.

If you have a choice of the litter, try to avoid the puppy that hides in the corner and seems reluctant to come to you. At the same time, the bold, dominant leader-type could well be a handful as he matures. The best choice is the middle-of-the-road puppy. Where

possible, try to take an experienced person with you to help you make the choice.

Many people advocate character-testing the puppies. This is a special test which claims to give an indication of the puppy's character. I would not presume to

The puppy you choose should be friendly and outgoing.

decry these tests, but I believe that, to be able to interpret the reactions of the pups to the test, one needs insight and experience with puppies. If you have this experience, you do not need a formal test, just observing and studying the litter should be enough.

The breeder should allow you to visit the pups several times, and, if you are unsure, do not choose one. There will be other litters.

PREPARATIONS

Assuming that you have made your choice, and your puppy will soon be arriving, it is time to start making preparations. There are lots of things to buy: a collar and lead, food and water dishes, toys, the list is endless. There are also many decisions to be made: where he will sleep, what he will eat, will he be allowed the run of the house, and many, many more.

Most of these decisions are a matter of personal choice, and it would be wrong of me to tell you that you must do this, or you must never do that. For example, I hear many people say that the dog must never be allowed to lie on the sofa. I disagree; let him lie on the sofa if that is what you want. But do not get angry when he lies

on that same sofa while covered in mud. Consistency is the key word. If the dog is not allowed in the sitting-room, then he should never be allowed in. Do not allow him in while your spouse is out, and then tell him off when he attempts to enter the room when your in-laws are visiting.

Plan beforehand what you want from your dog, and then start as you mean to go on. This does not mean that you cannot change your mind, but to keep changing it will only confuse and worry the dog. All dogs must have a secure and consistent life. They should have their own place, somewhere in the house that is warm in winter and cool in summer, where they can go if they want to have peace and quiet, and where we can put them if we want the same. So, make these plans, and buy some equipment, before the puppy arrives. I suggest the following:

INDOOR KENNEL OR CRATE

Your dog will need a place to sleep. When he first arrives at his new home a puppy may feel insecure and lonely. He will be separated from everything that he has known in his short life, so you must take the place of his mother, brothers and sisters. For the first

The indoor crate is an invaluable item of equipment.

few weeks I allow the puppy to sleep next to my bed. Years ago, I believed that if we allowed the puppy to sleep in the bedroom, he would never accept sleeping anywhere else. This is just not true. I have an indoor collapsible kennel which is put next to my bed at night, and taken downstairs each morning. The puppy sleeps happily in his kennel next to the bed for the first few weeks, and has his naps in it downstairs during the day. At about four months of age, once the puppy is completely settled into his new home, I just leave the kennel

downstairs one night. I have never had problems with the transition from bedroom to downstairs, and the puppy sleeps in his own 'room' each night.

The indoor kennel has other advantages:

• During the first week or two, while the puppy is being house trained, you can confine him in the kennel if you are too busy to watch him. If he wakes and needs to go out, he will soon let you know.

• If you have to leave him alone for a few hours, as we all have to from time to time, or are too busy to keep an eye on him, you can pop him into his kennel, secure in the knowledge that he is safe and cannot get up to mischief.

• When you go visiting, take the kennel with you, and the puppy can stay near you without the risk that he will mess on your mother-in-law's carpet.

COLLAR AND LEAD

Do not spend a lot of money buying an expensive collar and lead for a young puppy. They grow so fast that you will have to buy several before the dog reaches maturity. I prefer a simple nylon, or soft leather, collar and lead and very small puppies are often better off with a cat collar to start with.

I never allow a slip chain or half check on a puppy. In fact, I prefer a simple leather collar, even for adult dogs. I can accept that a five-foot-two lady with a two-year-old Rottweiler probably feels that a check chain may be more effective, but it is not the equipment that matters, rather, how it is used. Young dogs have very sensitive necks that can easily be damaged by check chains, even in the most careful hands.

A simple leather or rope lead, about a metre long, will do to start off with. Any longer will just get in the way. I do recommend an expandable Flexi-lead as they allow a dog some freedom while maintaining control of the untrained dog.

TOYS

We have all seen the child that gets an expensive toy as a Christmas present, and then proceeds to play with the box it came in. Dogs are no different. There must be hundreds of toys around our house, but the puppies always seem to prefer the newspaper, or a

There is a vast range of collars and leads to choose from.

If you catch your puppy chewing something he is not allowed, quickly swap the forbidden article for one of his own toys.

shoe. Play should be encouraged as it is a very important part of a dog's development, but the only way to make sure that a puppy plays with the toys that are intended for him is to keep everything else out of his reach. If you catch the puppy chewing on something that is not for chewing, pick up a toy that he can chew, and 'swap' him like for like. Do not panic or shout at him, as that will not teach him not to chew; it will only teach him to do it when you are not about.

Next time, remember to tidy up after you, or if the puppy is unsupervised, you could also place him in his kennel out of the way of temptation.

FOOD DISHES
Two dishes will be needed, one for food, and another for water. I prefer stainless steel dishes as they are durable and easy to clean. For the first few weeks an old plate or soup bowl will do, as the size of dish needed for an adult dog will be too big for a young puppy, and puppy dishes will soon be too small for the growing dog.

BLANKET AND BED
All puppies need to be kept warm, and an old blanket can be used for this purpose. There are special dog blankets on the market, and the better-quality ones help dry the

You will need two bowls – the stainless steel type is durable and easy to clean.

Dog chews are a great favourite.

dog if he has been wet. This material is also easily washed, and dries quickly.

Whatever you choose, it is best to take it with you when you go to pick up the puppy from the breeder. Leave the blanket on the floor and let all the puppies and the bitch play with it. You can use this blanket as a comforter when you take the puppy away from the litter as it will have the smell of his littermates and mother on it, which will make his leaving less traumatic. The blanket can then be placed in his kennel at night to help him adjust to his new home.

DOG CHEWS
Puppies love to chew, just like babies, so a selection of dog chews should always be at hand to occupy the dog if he has to be left alone. Some dogs love chewing while others are less enthusiastic, so it is worthwhile experimenting with several types to see which your dog prefers.

Apart from these necessities, there are lots of other things to buy the puppy that are great fun, and completely unnecessary. But who cares, its part of the fun!

BE CONSISTENT
Decisions also have to be made about where the dog will sleep once he is adjusted to the house, where he will do his toilet as a puppy, and as an adult dog, where he will be fed, and where he will stay when he comes in filthy and wet.

Once again, each situation is different, and a matter of personal choice, but try to be consistent. If you have bought an indoor kennel most of these problems are easily solved, as the dog can be fed in there (this will help him accept the kennel), it can become his place to sleep throughout his life, and it can be used as a holding area when he comes in wet and dirty. However, it is better to make a habit of always feeding the dog in the kennel, and always putting him in his kennel after a walk, even if he is dry, for a few

Take your puppy out and about so that he gets used to all the sights and sounds of a busy urban environment.

minutes. In this way, the dog knows his routine, and will accept it without protest.

HOUSE TRAINING

House training a young puppy can be very traumatic for the owner, if the dog is allowed the run of the house. By confining the puppy while unsupervised, and letting him out frequently, house training should only take a week or two. It is advisable to choose a quiet corner of the garden for the puppy to use as a toilet. As he gets older he can be taken further away, but initially the puppy has to urinate so often that there is really no alternative to the garden. I know of people who have trained their dog to use the cat-tray, but they have a Yorkshire Terrier. This would hardly be feasible for a Great Dane.

SOCIALISING

Perhaps the most important task you will have to undertake is to make sure that your puppy is fully socialised. It has been scientifically proved that well-socialised puppies have a far greater chance to grow into normal, well-balanced, adult dogs. The dictionary explains socialisation as 'adapting to social environment' and it is important that you give your dog plenty of opportunity to come into contact with all the things that he will have to accept in later life. All being well, the breeder will have started the process by introducing him to adults, children, the house, garden, and, perhaps, by taking him for a short ride in the car. Your job will be to continue this task by taking him into town, and letting him see crowds, traffic, other animals, hear strange noises and so on. In the house he should be introduced to the television, vacuum cleaner, washing machine etc. In the park he should meet joggers, cyclists, children playing games, dogs and other animals; the list is endless.

My dogs have been brought up in the country, and behave well with other animals and country life in general. However, as young dogs, they were taken into town as part of their socialisation. You should try to think of every eventuality and give your dog experience of any situations that he may encounter in later life.

One of the dilemmas the new puppy owner is confronted with is conflicting advice received on one the hand from people like myself, who counsel taking the puppy out into public as soon as possible, while on the other hand your veterinary surgeon may advocate isolating the puppy until he is fully inoculated, which may be as late as sixteen weeks of age. Both arguments are valid. However, you can carry the puppy in your arms in public, which will give him the chance to observe and absorb lots of new experiences, with only minimal risk.

A well-socialised dog will take all new experiences in his stride.

3 *Understanding Your Dog*

Dogs are gregarious animals, and need the contact and social interaction that results from being part of a family. Without this contact, dogs can develop abnormal behavioural habits that are unacceptable to the owner. The dog then becomes the proverbial 'problem dog', which results in it either being re-homed, given to the local animal shelter, or put down. In some cases a situation develops where both canine and human family members live from crisis to crisis, with neither enjoying the quality of life they have a right to. Almost all behaviour problems with dogs can be avoided if three basic rules are adhered to:

• Care is taken to select a dog of the right type, size, and more importantly, character, to suit the family he will be joining.

• The new owners take the time and trouble to learn the basics of how the canine mind works, and how a dog learns.

• All members of the new family are prepared to devote time and energy to teaching the new addition the house rules, and to actively participate in training and socialising the dog.

The dog owner should have an understanding of how the canine mind works.

PRACTICE MAKES PERFECT

In an ideal world, a potential dog owner would have experience of how to look after and care for a dog before actually owning one. You can, to a certain extent, gain some experience by offering to look after the pet of a family member or friend while they are on holiday, or you can join the local dog training club and attend as a spectator for a few months. This gives you the advantage of watching other people training their dogs without the stress and distraction of trying to control your own little terror. You may even decide, after a few visits, that you are not suited to owning a dog, after all. If, however, after attending classes, you are still convinced that you want a dog, you will have gained enough theoretical experience to give you and your new dog a good start in your life together. Sadly, I rarely see an owner at class until he or she already has a dog, and, as often as not, they do not join a class until problems have already developed. Prevention is better than a cure, and it is the responsibility of every dog owner to seek advice before behaviour problems arise. Dog clubs are so popular that there is sure to be one in your area, where the instructors will be more than willing to advise on the most suitable dog for you. Getting the right advice beforehand, and then seeking help and assistance once you have made your choice, is only common sense.

HOW DOGS LEARN

Dogs learn by association and experience. If a dog makes the association between a particular event and pleasure, he will, if the event is repeated several times, learn to anticipate the event, and will show his enjoyment. The most obvious example of this is mealtimes. The moment that we walk to the cupboard to prepare his food, the dog gets up to follow us, wagging his tail. We do not have to tell the dog it is dinner time; he has read the signs, associated them with previous experiences, and knows what is coming. This simplified example of how a dog reacts becomes slightly more complex when we realise that we may go to the cupboard many times each day without the dog reacting. How then does the dog know which of these times signals his mealtime?

Few dogs look forward to a visit to the vet. In fact, most dogs

Association and experience are key factors in learning.

become quivering wrecks just sitting in the waiting room. Is it really because they have been hurt by the wicked man with the needle? Of course not; most dogs do not even feel the slight pain of an injection. But still, most dogs hate going to the vet, even after only one or two visits, when nothing painful has happened. I have tried taking my dogs along to the vet just for a pat and tidbit, and the vet comes to my house to have coffee, not to treat the dogs. They still hate him after just one or two such meetings. How then does the dog know that this man may hurt him, even though he almost never does?

I believe that the dog anticipating his mealtime, and anticipating pain at the hands of the vet, is due to the canine ability to read and react to the most subtle combination of sounds, smells, and body language. This ability is far more developed in dogs than in humans. We often hear comments such as "Dogs can sense fear in a person". He does not have to sense it, he can see it, and he can smell it.

BODY LANGUAGE
If we are aware of the dog's highly developed ability to read subtle

changes in body language, or tone of voice, we can begin to understand why a normally obedient dog will sometimes disobey a command that he would usually react to. An example may clarify this: You are walking in the park with the dog running free, twenty or thirty yards ahead. You decide to change direction and call the dog's name with the command "Come". The dog reacts immediately, and takes the new direction as intended. This may happen several times during the walk, with the dog reacting as requested each time. Suddenly, you see a strange dog in the distance and decide to call your dog back to avoid possible problems. You call his name, with the command "Come", only to find that he does not react. You try to enforce your will upon the dog by repeating the command, this time with a little more force in your voice – no reaction. To make matters worse, you then start to shout and threaten, which gets the dog's attention, but he has no intention of coming any nearer.

We have all experienced this, or a similar, situation. Why does our normally obedient dog occasionally have these disobedient turns, and why must he always have them when there are other people and dogs about? The answer, of course, lies in ourselves. The dog is only reacting to previous experiences. He has realised that, if there is nothing particularly interesting about, we call him in a normal tone of voice, but the moment there is something of interest, we change our tone. That is his signal to look for the distraction that we have

Dogs have an uncanny understanding of body language.

already seen. He knows, from past experience, that "Come" in one tone means, "Come to Daddy", but if the tone is altered, "Come" means something completely different.

ASSOCIATION TRAINING

The ability to associate certain events with pleasant, or unpleasant, experiences can be put to good use during the upbringing and training of a dog. This does not mean that we should just praise or punish a dog depending on the lesson to be learnt. The dog learns from experience, and associates this experience with either pleasure, or discomfort. For instance, when training a puppy to accept his indoor kennel, we could pop him in it, close the door, and sit for hours, praising him in a friendly voice. It will not make him like the kennel. However, if we give him his meals in the kennel, with the door open so that he can leave at any time, he will soon learn that the kennel is where he gets his meals, and will willingly enter it without being . told.

Another example is the dog that sleeps in your favourite armchair. You can tell him off as much as you want, it will not stop him.

However, if you remove the cushions and replace them with an old pillowcase filled with uncomfortable things, such as wire brushes, bricks and other hard objects, the dog will learn, after two or three attempts, that he just cannot get comfortable, and will find somewhere else to snooze.

In both of these examples the dog has taught himself, by personal experience, and we have merely created the right situation for him to be able to learn. If this principle is understood, and is combined with a fertile imagination, most problems can be resolved quite easily.

DOMINANCE

The dog is a pack animal, and as such, must either have a pack leader, or will attempt to be the leader himself. He can also be completely happy in either role, so long as his place in the pack is clearly defined. In modern society it is unthinkable to allow a dog to be pack leader, and this role must be assumed by a family member, with the dog having the lowest position in the pecking order. Many of the problems that I see with so-called problem dogs are caused by the dog assuming a dominant position in the family

Small children should be supervised when playing with dogs.

hierarchy, or by the dog's place in the hierarchy not being clearly defined. Children are often the cause of pecking order problems, simply because they are seen as puppies by the family dog and, as such, will be accepted and tolerated by him. However, puppies have to be reprimanded from time to time, and they also have to be taught the rules of correct behaviour. If the parents, or pack leaders, fail to do this, the dog often will, resulting in the dog being blamed for reacting, to his way of thinking, in a completely natural way. For this reason, dogs and children should never be left alone together without supervision. Young children, in the pre-school stage, are especially at risk as they are unable to recognise the warning that a dog gives prior to actually snapping or biting. As with people, some dogs are extremely tolerant of children, while others have a short fuse. However, if a dog bites a child there is really only one person to blame, and that is the owner, or pack leader, who allowed the situation to arise. Every dog has the inherent ability to bite if the situation is wrong. However, with a thorough understanding of the dog's character, combined with correct socialisation and training, the average dog will go through life without causing a problem.

GETTING ADVICE

Aggressiveness and biting are only two of the behaviour problems that a dog can develop. Far more common are destructiveness, barking, chasing, fighting, urinating and defecating in the home, and many more. All of these problems are almost always caused by owner ignorance, and can be avoided, or cured, with proper knowledge and advice.

While it is very important to have a basic understanding of how the canine mind works, take care not to go overboard by psychoanalysing every movement or thought the dog has. Rearing a dog to become a social member of the family is mainly common sense.

Over the last few years dog training has developed into a profession, with canine-behaviour therapists becoming commonplace, and the techniques used in training dogs have become much more humane than the old-fashioned 'shout and jerk' method. However, for the inexperienced dog owner, it is often impossible to determine where to go for the best advice. Many trainers and therapists have gone from one extreme to the other, and are telling dog owners that a dog must never be castigated for bad behaviour. I believe this is potentially just as dangerous as overcorrection. A sharp reprimand for unacceptable behaviour is an integral part of rearing a puppy, and failure to do so at the correct moment will lead to dominance problems later on.

UNDERSTANDING TRAINING

Training a dog can be split into two categories:
The teaching of good behaviour.
The removal of (potentially) bad behaviour.

Teaching a dog a new command

Social interaction between littermates is made up of play and squabbles.

can be done without the use of force and correction. However, when discouraging bad habits or unacceptable behaviour, I see no problem in physically reprimanding a puppy if this is done with minimal force, and the puppy has ignored a verbal warning. If you observe a bitch with pups, you will see that the first time she reprimands a puppy she snaps at it quite sharply, usually causing the puppy to squeal in shock and pain, and then she will growl. The next time, the growl is enough.

If we want to correct a dog by saying "No" to forbid an action, we first have to teach the pup the meaning of the command "No". The first time I correct a puppy, I either give him a shake, or a two-fingered slap on the snout, while saying "No", in a stern voice. The puppy quickly understands that "No" is a reprimand, and I then use that word if I want to admonish the puppy. The physical reprimand, together with a verbal correction, should only be needed once or twice for the dog to understand and react to the verbal command alone. However, I only use a physical reprimand if the puppy is showing dominance, or aggressive behaviour. It should never be used for the puppy failing to obey a command such as "Sit", or "Come", or if he urinates on the floor.

By studying a litter of puppies we can see that play and squabbles are a major part of the social interaction between members of the litter. We also see a pecking order developing, although this order can change from day to day, until such time as it is firmly established. If there is a clearly defined top dog in the litter, this dog should be avoided for the average family home. However, even the most submissive dog will try to take top place if the new owner gives in during conflict situations. I frequently receive calls from distraught owners who have been attacked by their dogs, and find that the 'attacker' is an eight or nine-week-old terrorist in the making. This is not unnatural behaviour. All puppies try to get their own way by the use of force, and most will 'try it on'. If he sees any hesitation or fear in the owner, any puppy will soon learn that a growl or a bite will allow him to get his own way.

CONTROLLING PLAY

Most puppies go to their new homes at about eight weeks of age, and by this time will be active for about three hours each day. Much of this activity will be taken up by play, which should be encouraged, with the owner initiating and ending the play period. By the use of play, the pecking order can be determined, with the owner taking the dominant role. During play you should determine who does what, and if the puppy gets too boisterous, the play session should be interrupted until the puppy calms down. In this way the puppy will learn to control himself and accept leadership.

Play consists mainly of tug-of-war and games of 'catch me if you can'. When playing tug-of-war, make sure that the puppy loses more than he wins, as this proves to him that you are superior. I find it helps if you have two of each type of toy. If the puppy has one, and you think that you cannot get it away from him, start to play with the other and he will release the one he has, in an attempt to get yours. As he does so, say "Leave", and then let him have your toy. You can then pick up the toy he has dropped, and keep repeating the swap. In this way you always take the initiative and dictate the play, while the puppy learns that you are the source of the game, not the toy.

With 'catch me if you can', the dog will try to tease you into chasing him to get the toy. This is acceptable in moderation, but once again, by use of the other toy you can reverse the roles and get the dog to chase you, thereby always keeping the initiative. This sort of guided play will assist the puppy in realising that you are in charge.

BE FIRM

Puppies can get over-excited, and may nip you quite painfully. If this happens, do not yelp in pain and fear as this teaches the puppy that he can win, and is capable of hurting you. Firmly, but without frightening him, let him know that biting hurts and is not allowed, and stop the play for a few seconds. He will have experienced when playing with his littermates that, if he plays too rough, the play session will end, and he will have learned to moderate his actions.

Children should be carefully watched when playing with a puppy, as they tend to squeal and shriek a lot if bitten, even playfully. This only excites the puppy and makes things worse. Play should be encouraged, but make sure that you are the one who always ends the play session, once again proving your dominance.

Play is used to build up a good relationship, and to define who is boss.

4 Basic Training

Training can be divided into two sections; obedience training, which includes teaching commands such as "Sit", "Come", "Down", etc., and behaviour training, which is the defining of rules of what is, or is not, allowed. This includes such things as not sleeping on the bed, nor chasing the cat, nor being fed tidbits from the table, and so on. Many people often confuse these two elements so I give the following example to clarify matters. A dog that wants to chase sheep but does not do so, is a well-trained dog. However, the dog that has been reared not to want to chase sheep, is a well-behaved dog. There is a subtle, but very important, difference.

Dogs must be taught a certain amount of basic obedience training. Just how much training a dog needs depends upon the home situation. However, I think all dogs need to be taught the commands "Come", "Sit", "Down", and "Stay", and to walk on a loose lead. This is a minimum requirement, and all dogs benefit from being well trained and well-behaved.

I always recommend that a dog should attend puppy classes, followed by basic obedience classes. Not only will the inexperienced owner receive help and advice on training, but also the dog will become socialised with other dogs and people, which will, in turn, improve his behaviour and attitude in public. However one hour per week at the dog training club will not be enough to train the dog. Obedience training must be taught daily, while behaviour training is something that must be constantly taught, and reinforced, every moment you are with the dog. It would be pointless to train the dog for a half-an-hour each day, and then let him run free and be a nuisance for the rest of the day, ignoring all lessons taught in the training session.

Training should start from the moment your puppy arrives home.

PUPPY TRAINING

Training your puppy should begin immediately, as he will be learning during every waking moment, and either he will learn what you want him to, or he will learn something else.

Puppies can be very time-consuming, and the first few weeks will, to a certain extent, determine your relationship with the dog for the rest of his life. You will be taking the place of the puppy's mother, so it is up to you to educate your dog in the rules of life. Normally, his mother would clean up after him until he is old enough to leave the nest, and imitate and learn from her where he should go to the toilet. You will have to take over this role and must teach the puppy where to do his toilet. At first he will make mistakes, but when this happens he must never be corrected, even if he is caught in the act. Just clean up after him, and by watching him carefully you will soon learn to recognise the warning signs, then pick him up, take him to the chosen place, and wait for him to do the business. As he does so, give him a command such as "Be clean", or any phrase you choose. If you do this every time, and praise him for going, he will soon get the idea and start to go on command. You will also start to recognise that puppies soon get into a routine in their day-to-day life, including going to the toilet.

Generally your puppy will urinate immediately after waking up, after eating, and following a play session, as well as countless other times, and you should anticipate this and take him outdoors in good time. For the first week or two the puppy should be taken out every half-an-hour, unless he is sleeping. How often he defecates is often determined by the type of food, and how many meals, he has, but you will soon see the routine. Most puppies should be house-trained within a week to ten days, barring the occasional accident.

For the first few nights the puppy may not sleep the whole night through, and if he awakens he should be let out, which is why I let my puppies sleep at the side of my bed – I should say, on my wife's side. I find that puppies start to sleep the whole night through within a week or two.

The indoor kennel is an invaluable aid to house training a young puppy. A dog will never foul his own bed if he can avoid doing so, and therefore, confining the puppy for short periods, when you cannot give him attention, will help avoid mistakes. The kennel will help in all sorts of situations when the puppy cannot be allowed to run free around the house.

INDOOR KENNELS

Some people disagree with the use of an indoor kennel, believing that it is cruel to confine a puppy to such a small area. These same people have a clear conscience when putting a baby in a cot surrounded with bars, or in his play-pen, which has similar constraints. If trained in the correct way, the puppy will come to regard his kennel as his own little room, and will show no resentment.

Your puppy should be introduced to the kennel gradually. For the first few times he enters the kennel, the door should be left open so that he does not feel trapped, and can leave if he wants. You can throw a few tidbits in, and encourage him to go in and get them. If he is sleepy, gently pick him up and place him in the kennel, but leave the door open. He should also receive his meals in the kennel. Gradually you can close the door for a few minutes, perhaps giving him a chew or suchlike to keep him occupied, and making sure that you always stay in the room. In this way the puppy will quickly become acclimatised and accept confinement.

The most common mistake that is made is to dump the puppy in the kennel for the first time, and then leave him alone for a few hours. This can be very traumatic and may result in the puppy regarding the kennel as a canine prison cell, which is the last thing you want.

COLLAR AND LEAD

The new puppy will also have to accept wearing a collar, often with a lead attached. Most puppies resent a collar being placed around the neck, but soon become used to it.

There is a very simple method that will avoid any struggle to get the collar on for the first time. Make sure that the collar is large enough to fit easily over the puppy's head. With the collar in one hand, attract the puppy's attention by offering him a tidbit. Once the puppy is interested, place the hand holding the tidbit through the loop of the collar, and offer it to the puppy. As he attempts to take it, withdraw your

The collar must be large enough to fit over the dog's head.

hand and encourage the puppy to follow the tidbit through the collar. As the puppy places his head through the collar reward him with the tidbit, and take the collar off again.

Repeat this several times before you attempt to leave the collar on. Once the puppy accepts the collar, let him wear it for a minute or two, gradually increasing the time until he does not react to wearing it.

You can now attach the lead to the collar. To start with, it is a good idea to attach the lead, and then distract the dog by having a game with his favourite toy. In this way he will probably not even realise that the lead is attached. Once he is used to wearing both lead and collar, he can be taken into the garden for a game. After a few days you can begin the lead training as described below. However, do not be in a hurry to take your young puppy into the street as he will tire very quickly, and does not need long walks, so lead training in the garden is enough for the first few weeks.

Do not make the mistake of putting your puppy on the lead and immediately taking him out for a walk. This can be a very traumatic experience for a young

Offer a tidbit while holding the collar over the nose.

As the dog places his head through the collar, reward with a tidbit.

dog. From his point of view, he cannot understand why this strange object is placed around his neck, which is then used to pull him out into the big bad world. This may sound logical, but many, otherwise sensible, people do just this, and cannot understand why their dog resents being walked on the lead. Luckily for us, dogs are such forgiving creatures.

OPPORTUNITY TRAINING

Young puppies learn surprisingly quickly, and basic obedience training should begin from the first day. I start obedience training in a very simple way, which I call opportunity training. Every time that the puppy does something, which will later be part of his formal training, I give him the appropriate command together with lots of verbal praise, and a tidbit which I always have in my pocket.

For instance, if the puppy sits, I would say "Sit. What a clever boy", or if he runs up to me, I would give the "Come" command, together with lots of praise. In this informal way, the puppy soon associates the command with the action. This principle is not restricted to obedience commands. If the dog enters his kennel, I will say "Go in your kennel"; if he barks, I will say "Speak"; and when he stops barking, I will say "Quiet".

Any action the dog makes, that you may want him to do on command later in life, should be given a name. This preparation work will make further training much easier, as the puppy will not only have learnt some of the commands, he will have heard these commands while doing something of his own free will, and will soon realise that he is rewarded for doing so. This

method develops the so-called 'will to please'.

A young puppy of only eight weeks is quite capable of learning basic obedience commands such as "Sit", "Down", "Stand", "Come", and so on. The method of teaching this is, in principle, the same for a puppy or an adult dog.

BEHAVIOUR TRAINING

To avoid confusion, I should explain again the difference between obedience training and behaviour training. Obedience training will teach the dog to obey

Your dog must learn the house rules – and you must be consistent in applying them in all situations.

certain commands such as "Sit", "Down", and "Come". In other words, the dog will do what he is told, when commanded to do so.

Behaviour training entails educating the dog to conform to a certain code of behaviour without being told. Toilet training, not begging at the table, not lying on the bed, not jumping up at visitors, and suchlike, are typical examples.

I cannot imagine that any dog owner would want their dog to chase cars, or bite the postman, so this type of unacceptable behaviour is universally frowned upon. However, there are other canine activities that are welcomed by some people, while being suffered by others. Many people are happy to sit watching television while sharing an armchair with their beloved pet, while other owners do not even allow their dog in the sitting-room. This is a matter of personal preference. As long as you are consistent in laying down the rules of behaviour your dog will learn to accept them, and will obey them. Problems arise when the dog is invited on to the sofa one day, but punished when he is caught taking a nap there the next.

CREATURES OF HABIT

Dogs are creatures of habit and routine, and will adapt to almost any situation as long as there are clearly defined rules. Therefore, I always advise dog owners to decide on a list of 'Do's and Don'ts' for their pet before he arrives, making sure that all members of the family are aware of what will be allowed, and what will not, to ensure that they start as they mean to go on.

A dog that begs at the table during mealtimes does so because he has learnt that by doing so he will receive a reward. A dog that never receives a tidbit during mealtimes will soon learn that there is no point in begging, and will cease to do so. However, if he occasionally gets the odd morsel, even from only one particular person, he will always attempt to beg. If the dog is commanded to "Go and lie down", on such occasions, and obeys this command, it only proves that he is obedient. He will still return to the table at the next mealtime. The dog that does not beg in the first place is the well-behaved dog.

On this point, I should say that all my dogs beg at mealtimes. This is because my wife and I do not mind the dogs begging to share our meal. Such behaviour only becomes a problem when the dog does something that is objectionable to his owner.

INHERITED TRAITS

All behaviour that a dog exhibits is either inherited or taught. If you decide to buy a Border Collie you can reasonably expect him to show some form of his inherited instinct to herd. It is common to see a Collie herding his family while walking in the park, running around and around the family group, or running ahead and laying down, only to run or a few yards further to lay down again, as the family approaches. This behavioural instinct, although quite normal in a Collie, can become obsessive, and therefore, should be suppressed from the outset – unless you are willing to accept it.

We have four Border Collies; Woolie, who is twelve, Dazzle six, Scully three, and lastly Stevie, the baby, at eighteen months. On our daily walks, Dazzle shadows every move that Woolie makes; he, in turn, is shepherded by Scully, who

The Border Collie has an inherited instinct to herd – but you must control the extent to which this affects behaviour patterns.

attempts to prevent Dazzle from leading the walk. Stevie guards Scully, making sure that he stays with the group. Because we live in the country, and the dogs can run free, this behaviour is not a problem, and so we allow it. In another situation this (from the dogs' point of view) normal act could become a problem, and we would not have allowed it to develop.

We have another dog, an eight-year-old German Shepherd called Kelsey, who will have nothing to do with such silly games, and shows no aptitude to herd. We also have three sheep, and none of our Collies shows the slightest interest in herding them, because they were taught not to do so as young puppies. They now ignore the sheep completely.

From the above example, it can be seen that inherited traits have to be combined with opportunity to become a habit. Our dogs have the inherited trait to herd, and by allowing them to herd each other, we gave them the opportunity, so this became a habit. We never gave them the opportunity to herd the sheep, so this inherited trait has been suppressed to such a degree that they no longer show any interest.

TAUGHT BEHAVIOUR

When selecting a dog, consideration should be given to the character and potential inherited instincts that the dog may exhibit. Once the choice has been made, care should be taken to suppress unacceptable behaviour before this develops. However, most behaviour habits, both good and bad, are taught.

Be consistent in your training. If you have allowed your dog to jump up, do not tell him off when he does so with muddy paws and you are wearing your best clothes.

A typical example of taught behaviour that is welcomed at first, only to be frowned upon at a later stage, is when a dog jumps up, attempting to lick the face of anyone he meets. Most probably, this dog was picked up and cuddled as a small puppy, and was encouraged to lick the face, and held in the arms, many times each day. But puppies grow up, and suddenly the taught behaviour becomes a problem, and the dog is punished for attempting to do something that he had previously been actively encouraged to do.

It is not wrong to pick puppies up and cuddle them; in fact it is extremely important that puppies are handled and petted. We should realise, however, that the dog will learn to enjoy this activity, even when he gets older, and it is wrong to punish a dog for attempting to do something that we have taught him to do. If you do not want a dog to jump up, he should be taught not to do so. I see many people who allow their dogs to jump up when the owners are wearing old clothes, only to scream at the dogs if they attempt to do so when their owners are wearing a suit or a smart dress. This is confusing and stressful to the dogs.

SETTING HOUSE RULES

Behaviour training is a matter of deciding what is acceptable behaviour that suits your particular needs, and then consistently teaching your dog the clearly defined rules. I willingly admit that my dogs behave in a way that probably would be unacceptable to the average family. This is because my life revolves around dogs, and they play a major role in my life. It would be wrong of me to suggest that your dog should be allowed on the bed, or that you should feed the dog from the table at mealtimes. My advice is to decide what you require from your dog and be consistent in applying the rules. For the new, inexperienced dog owner, there are, however, certain guidelines that should be adhered to.

In the house, decide upon any 'No go' areas, such as bedrooms, sitting-room, and so on, and then prevent the dog from ever entering these areas, either by always closing the door, or putting up a child gate. Do not expect an untrained dog not to enter an area just because you have corrected him a few times. A dog that is punished for lying on the sofa will, at best, learn not to do so

The dog must learn to fit in with the family situation, understanding his place in the pecking order.

when you are in the room. He will soon realise that he is only punished for lying on the sofa when you are there. When he is alone he is not corrected, and will soon realise that he is punished when he attempts to lie on the sofa only when you are about, so will not do so in your presence. He will not understand that he must never lie on the furniture, and you will come home to a dog that is lying innocently in his basket, but you will still have a hairy sofa.

Decide where the dog will sleep, and where he will receive his meals. This should be a place that is warm in the winter, cool in the summer, and quiet enough to ensure that he will not be constantly under your feet. Although a dog must have his own place in the house, he should be allowed a certain amount of freedom. Dogs need social contact, and should not be isolated from the rest of the family. It would be wrong to expect a dog to spend endless hours alone in one small restricted area, such as a shed, or the utility room. A dog should be part of the family, and he should be allowed to join in family activities, as he is a social animal and needs company.

If your dog has been trained to accept the confines of an indoor kennel, you can avoid so many potential problems by putting him in there if you are too busy to give him attention, or if he has to be alone. Almost all of the most common problems that occur in the house, such as unwanted chewing and destructiveness, can be avoided if the dog has a kennel.

All dogs need to be exercised, and part of the pleasure of owning a dog is taking him for a walk. A well-behaved, trained dog, is a pleasure to own. Once again, any problems, such as a dog pulling on the lead, or not coming back during the daily walks, are caused by lack of obedience training, or more commonly, by incorrect upbringing, resulting in behaviour problems. A major part of a puppy's education is socialisation, bringing him into contact with all the things that he will encounter in his daily life. Other dogs and animals, people, traffic, joggers, cyclists, the list is endless. If a puppy is introduced to, and accepts, all these new experiences at an early age, he will learn to accept and, therefore, ignore them.

Obedience Exercises

Once you have established 'house rules' with your dog it is important to graduate to teaching some basic obedience exercises. These do not have to be conducted with competition style precision (unless you have ambitions in that area), but you are looking for a swift response to the commands you give.

LEAD WALKING

Many dog owners are happy to have a dog that does not pull on the lead, rather than a dog that walks to heel. Initially, teaching a dog not to pull is sufficient, and it is not really necessary to make a dog walk constantly next to the leg. If you are in the park with plenty of open space, the lead can

Your dog must learn to walk on a loose lead without resistance.

Choose a distraction-free area for training, and keep sessions short.

personal preference, but if you attend dog training classes, this will be the preferred side.

I start all training in the garden, where I teach my dogs to walk, on the lead without pulling, before taking them out onto the street. Start by placing the dog on the lead, and take him into the garden. Just walk about in the garden holding the end of the lead and watching the dog carefully. As the dog decides to head off in one direction, be ready to give a gentle tug on the lead just as the lead is about to tighten. At the same time, call his name, and head off in the opposite direction. It is not necessary to jerk your dog head over heels, a gentle tug will do. The dog will, most probably, turn and try to run ahead of you again. Repeat the tug, while calling the dog's name, and changing direction. Continue to do this until the dog begins to walk within the restriction of the loose lead, at which time you can praise him. Keep the session short, five minutes at a time, but preferably three or four times per day. Within a day or two the dog will realise what is required of him, and will stop pulling on the lead. It is important to keep changing direction at the exact moment that

be lengthened, and the dog allowed a certain amount of controlled freedom, walking on a loose lead, without pulling. If the dog is taken into town, the lead can be shortened, and the dog will walk closer to the handler. This is possible once the dog has been taught not to pull on the lead. It is generally accepted that the dog should walk on your left-hand side. This, of course, is a matter of the lead will tighten, and, as the training progresses, change direction at will, giving a tug on the lead at the correct moment. Do not keep talking to the dog to keep his attention, just call his name as you tug on the lead, and give a few words of praise when he walks on a loose lead.

Do not attempt to take the dog into the street until this lesson has been fully understood, and he can walk around the garden on a loose lead without attempting to pull. This should only take a day or two, and for this short period your dog should only be exercised, and go to the toilet, in the garden. Once the dog is walking on a loose lead in the garden he can be taken for a short, five-minute walk. Once again, the lesson he has been taught should be repeated in the street, and you should change direction every time he attempts to pull on the lead. As his training progresses, the duration of the walk can be gradually increased.

Consistency is the key word; a dog that is never allowed to pull on the lead will never attempt to do so. If you take the dog for an hour's walk, and ensure that he walks to heel on a loose lead for fifty-five minutes, and then let him

In competitive Obedience, the dog's attention is focused on the handler, but most owners do not aspire to this precision.

pull for the last five, he will learn that he can sometimes pull, and therefore will always try to do so. The secret is to never teach him to pull in the first place.

However, there is one situation where he should be allowed to pull, in moderation, and that is when he has to go to the toilet. Prior to urinating or defecating, a dog needs to sniff around to find a suitable place. To enable the dog to do this, you may have to let him pull you as he follows the 'scent' to his preferred place. Dogs can be taught to void on command, so I advise owners to select an area where the dogs can go to the toilet, and ensure that they walk there on a loose lead. The command is then given to "Be clean", or suchlike, and the dog is allowed to gently pull in that area only. Once he has done his business, he should be praised, and taken away from the area, once again resorting to the no-pull mode.

It is worth noting that, once a dog has learnt to pull on the lead, it can be hard to break the habit, and expert advice should be sought. However, all dogs can learn to walk on a loose lead, even after years of pulling. The difficulty is convincing the owner that his dog can be retrained. If I can get the doubtful owner to believe that he is capable of teaching his dog, he soon gets the confidence to carry on. I start by giving the owner a simple goal to achieve. He must try to walk a very short distance, perhaps between two lamp-posts, without the dog pulling. This should be done during the daily walk, and once they have achieved this, the

dog can go back to pulling, for the time being. Once the first goal is achieved he must set another, say, two lamp-posts, and so on. Gradually, the distance the dog goes while pulling is reduced, while the distance he walks without pulling is increased, until the dog can complete the entire walk on a loose lead. More importantly, the owner feels he has achieved something.

I willingly admit that this is not the optimum method for the dog, but I find that lack of success in training is caused, as often as not, by the owner believing that he is incapable of training his dog. By compromising, and setting easily attainable goals, we can overcome this problem.

THE RECALL

All dogs should return to their owner when told to do so. At obedience training clubs this is referred to as the Recall exercise, and the dog will be taught to run back to his owner, and sit in front in the 'present'. Whether the owner wants, or needs, such precision is a matter of personal preference. However, the ability to call the dog back to the owner anywhere, and anytime, is absolutely essential.

When calling your dog to you, give plenty of encouragement.

The easiest way to teach this command is for two family members to call the dog back and forwards between them to receive a reward. A few days' repetition of this will soon instil in the dog what is required.

Begin by taking the dog into the garden, or any other area that is enclosed, so that the dog cannot escape. One person should hold the dog while the other runs a few yards away. Then turn and call the dog in a friendly, excited voice, while holding a toy or a piece of food in clear view, to attract the dog's attention. The person holding the dog can then release him, while the other encourages him to come. Once the dog runs up to the other person he can be rewarded, and the first person can then call him back again for a reward, together with lots of verbal praise. In this way the dog can be called back and forth several times, each time receiving a reward. The dog will find this lots of fun and will soon learn to come when called.

This method works equally well for puppies or adult dogs. However, with small dogs or puppies it is advisable to start by kneeling on the ground, until the dog understands what is required of him. After a few days of this, the dog can be taken into the garden by just one person and allowed to run free. The dog can then be called back, rewarded, and immediately released. This Recall should be repeated several times each session so that the dog understands that being recalled does not necessarily mean that his freedom is over. He just runs up to his owner, receives praise and reward, and then can run off again.

The most common cause of a dog not returning when told is that he is only called back to his owner once each time he is free, when the walk is over, and he has to be put on the lead to return home. He soon realises that this means the end of freedom. By calling the dog back, rewarding him, and then letting him run off again, this problem can be avoided.

Once the dog is returning every time that he is called, he can be taken to a quiet place in the park and allowed to run free. The previous lesson can be repeated, with the dog being called back for a reward before being released again. If this lesson is repeated

throughout the dog's life, the problem of not coming when called should never develop. The mistake that many people make is to take the dog to the park and let him run free and do more or less whatever he wants. The dog is ignored until something (for the dog) interesting happens; he finds a jogger to chase, or a rabbit, or sees another dog in the distance. The moment something interests him, he is called back to the owner, and the dog soon realises that if the owner calls him there is something interesting about, but he must go back to be put on the lead. By calling the dog back as I describe, resentment at returning to the owner will not develop.

Adult dogs that are in the habit of not coming back when called, or dogs that are established chasers of rabbits, cats, joggers, or suchlike, fall into the category of problem dogs, and are less likely to react to this method, although it is certainly worth trying. Such dogs have already learned that, when running free, the owner has no control, and is in no position to prevent the chase. These dogs need special training, and help should be sought from an expert to increase the level of control over the dog.

STATIONARY COMMANDS

The ability to command a dog to "Lie down and stay" is extremely useful, and can be used in countless situations, such as when the house is full of visitors, or if you take the dog to visit other people, on the bus or train, and at the vet's surgery. Many people train their dogs to stay in both the Sit and the Down positions. However, for basic pet dog training, I prefer to make a distinction between a Stay command, where the dog must stay until I return to him, and a Wait command, when I may leave him and call him to me later. To avoid confusion, I teach my dogs to Sit and Wait prior to being called, but if I want the dog to Stay, I place him in the Down position. In this way the dog soon understands that he will never be called to me from the Down-stay, and is much more relaxed.

If you decide to go beyond basic pet dog training and enter obedience competitions, the dog will be expected to be called from the Down, and will also have to be taught a Sit-stay, as this is a required exercise. However, this book is about pet dogs and is not intended for anything more than basic training.

Once your dog has learnt the Sit command, you can delay giving the food reward – and even introduce some distractions!

THE SIT

As in all initial training, the dog should be taken to a quiet room, or into the garden, where there are no distractions. Put the dog on the lead and attract his attention by calling his name, and offering a tidbit. Hold the tidbit above his head and speak to him in an encouraging voice. At first the dog may jump up in an attempt to get the reward, in which case hold it just out of his reach. He will soon realise that he cannot get the food, and will go into the Sit position simply because he can see the food better from the Sit. As he does so, give the "Sit" command, together with the reward and verbal praise, and then release him from the Sit by saying "OK". Repeat this step several times in the first session. Within a day or two you will see that, the moment food is held above his head, the dog will go into the Sit in expectation of his reward. At this point you can start to give the "Sit" command prior to placing the food above his head. If the dog does not sit immediately do not give a second command, just hold the food above his head until he sits.

Do not get into the habit of giving more than one command. Once the dog is sitting every time that he is commanded, the hand signal, holding the reward, can be removed, and the food reward kept in a pocket, out of sight, and then given once the dog has obeyed the verbal command. As the dog gains experience the food reward can be dispensed with altogether, and just verbal praise given. However, I do suggest that the occasional food reward is given to reinforce the command and praise.

To encourage the dog to sit for longer periods, the food reward can be delayed for a few seconds before being given. This can gradually be built up until the dog will sit for half a minute or so before being released. I would not bother to teach the dog to sit for more than half a minute. If you want the dog to stay still for longer periods I would suggest that you place him in the Down, as he will be much more comfortable.

The Wait command should be taught progressively, gradually building up the distance you can leave your dog.

Once given the command to Wait, these dogs will not attempt to jump out until their leads have been attached.

THE WAIT

Once the dog is happily sitting on command, and will do so for about half a minute, you can start to teach the dog the Wait command. Begin with the dog in the Sit position. Stand in front of the dog and take a step to the right, while repeating the "Sit" command, and adding "Wait", all the time praising the dog in a calm voice. Then take a step to the left, while continuing to praise him for sitting. Return to the dog, and stand next to him on his right-hand side, before releasing him. From the initial two steps, gradually build up the distance that you leave the dog. You can circle round him, walk backwards to the end of the lead, and so on, talking to the dog in a calm, friendly voice all the time, while repeating the command, and praising him. Never call the dog to you at this stage. Leave him in the Sit until you can walk about ten steps away with the dog sitting happily.

Once he can do this, you can, if you want, call him to you with the aid of a tidbit. However, I would not advise you to call the dog every time, as he will soon start to anticipate the recall and become unsteady in the Sit. I would suggest calling him one time in five. In other words, leave the dog and return to him four times for every time that you call him. In this way you can avoid the dog anticipating. Do not correct the dog, or tell him off, if he does come without being called. A dog should never be told off for coming to you. Just repeat the basic exercise of leaving and returning to him, without calling him, a few more times. The distance that you leave your dog before calling him is a matter of personal preference. Just remember to build up gradually to maintain the dog's confidence.

One situation where the Wait command is invaluable is when the dog is travelling in the car. If the dog has been taught to do so, the Wait command can be given each time the door is opened. This will give you time to attach the lead and make sure the road is clear, before calling the dog out of the car. This exercise is extremely important for your dog's safety, and many a life has been lost by a dog jumping out of the car before being told to do so. At dog shows, all of my dogs sit in the car with the doors and tailgate open, and would never attempt to leave the car without being told to do so.

THE DOWN

The Down is a submissive position for a dog, which is why many people have trouble teaching it in group training classes. Many dogs are not at ease with other dogs in close proximity, and feel more secure standing or sitting. Therefore, once again, the ideal place to teach your dog the Down is in the garden, or in the house, with no distractions.

Start off by sitting on the ground, with one leg tucked up under your bottom. Make a bridge of your other leg by raising your knee. Place the dog on one side of your raised leg, and offer him a tidbit from the other side, by reaching through with your arm, under the raised leg. As the dog attempts to take the food, draw your arm slowly through and encourage the dog to follow the food. As he does so he will go into the Down position in an attempt to crawl under your raised knee to get the food. Once he is in the Down give the appropriate command, praise, reward and then release him. The dog will get the idea within a few minutes, and this step can be repeated several times in the first session. Once the dog is going down every time, the food can be placed on the ground as the dog goes under the leg, and you can cover the food with your hand for a second or two before removing it to let the dog take the food. After several sessions of this the leg can be removed and the dog will go down the moment he sees the hand signal containing the food on the floor.

As with teaching the Sit, the Down command should initially be given only once the dog is in the Down. After a few days of training, the command can be given prior to placing the hand on the floor, and the dog will start to go down on the verbal command, rather than the hand signal. It is important to get the timing right, so begin with the hand signal followed by the verbal command, then build up to the verbal command reinforced by the hand signal. Later on you can remove the hand signal altogether, if you wish.

In both the Sit and the Down the dog has been taught to react to a signal, and a verbal command. For pet dog training, I believe that the dog should always

Food is used to teach the Down, backed up with the verbal command.

*As your dog grows in confidence, you can increase
the duration of the Stay and attempt a group Stay.*

receive both commands, so that he will react to either. It takes no effort to give a hand signal while giving a command, and the dog has two chances to understand what is required of him. However, once again, the personal preference of the owner is the only consideration.

THE STAY

As with the Sit, the dog that has been taught the initial Down command must now learn to stay in the Down until released. The way to teach this is almost identical to teaching the Sit-and-Wait, except the dog will never be called from the Down. The owner should always return to the dog. Stay means just that, "Stay there, I will come back to you". Wait means "Wait there for the next command". I prefer to teach a Down-stay, and a Sit-wait.

When teaching the dog to Stay, great care must be taken to build the dog's confidence. The distance at which the dog is left should be gradually built up, with the owner returning to the dog time and again, to help him understand what is required. As the dog progresses, the duration of the Stay can be increased to five or even ten minutes, and the dog can even be left out of sight. To teach this, it is advisable to leave the dog in a secure place, while you go out of the dog's sight, but where you are still able to watch him; round the corner of a house, for instance. While standing out of sight of the dog, you should still occasionally praise him, and talk to him, so that he gets the idea that, even if he cannot see you, you are still around.

The above commands are the basic essentials required to control a dog in public places. More advanced training will certainly help you bond with your dog, and it is the success of this training that will decide whether your dog is going to be a liability or an asset. I would advise all puppy owners to attend training classes as early as possible, and to accept that for the first year they should attend a weekly course. This is not enough in itself – the lessons learned at training classes should be reinforced by daily practice at home. With regular practice, your dog will learn to obey quickly and willingly, and you will have the satisfaction of owning a pet that can be taken anywhere without embarrassment.

6 Problem Dogs

It can be said, with a certain amount of truth, that there are no problem dogs, only problem owners. However, once a dog has become a problem, the priority must be to find a cure, and placing the blame is of lesser importance. Although prevention is better than cure, this is of little solace to the owner of the dog, but training clubs and specialist behaviour therapists are more than willing to help those owners who are willing make the effort, and spend the time, to cure the problem. With careful guidance and advice almost all problems can be resolved, often very quickly and simply.

Some of the more common problems are fighting with other dogs, aggressiveness, destructiveness and chewing in the home, and barking, All of these problems can be cured. However, very often the owner is indirectly the cause of these problems in the first place, either by unwittingly encouraging the dog to commit the act, or by tolerating the problem until it becomes a habit.

BARKING

Most people want their dog to give a warning bark or two if someone approaches the house. They may even welcome more than one or two barks at night, or if the dog is alone in the house. After all, it is comforting to think that the family pet is also a watchdog and guardian. However, we tend to behave irrationally on this subject. If a suspicious character knocks on the door, we are pleased with Fido when he sounds fierce and intimidating. An hour later, we get very upset that Fido makes the same commotion when our boss arrives for dinner. Obviously, this can be very confusing for the dog, as he

The key to owning a well-behaved, well-adjusted dog is to provide a comprehensive programme of socialisation during his first twelve months.

cannot discriminate between friend and foe, as we can. He is limited to people he knows, and people he does not. To avoid this problem, we have to determine clear lines of behaviour for the dog to adhere to. In our house the rules are quite simple. If the dogs are in the company of myself or my wife, they do not have to bark, and if they do so they are told to be quiet, and "Quiet" is a command, not a reprimand. To teach them to be quiet we first had to teach them to bark, and once they barked on command they were taught to keep barking until told to stop. In this way, we are secure in the knowledge that our dogs will warn us of any

visitors, while, at the same time, the barking is controlled enough not to be a nuisance. This type of training is simple if the dog is trained before the bad habit develops. Retraining a problem dog is more difficult, as you are fighting against an inherent trait that has had the opportunity to develop into a habit.

To cure the problem we must first understand it from the dog's point of view. As an example, we can take the dog that is a postman-hater. Each day the dog hears someone approach the house, and he barks a warning. At first just a woof or two, but to his surprise this woof does the trick, and the intruder flees. This gives

A puppy will learn to cope with experiences that may at first appear daunting.

Socialising with other dogs and people is extremely important for breeds such as these German Shepherds which have inherant guarding instincts.

the dog confidence, and the next time the postman arrives the dog barks again, with the same success. Very soon, the habit is formed; the intruder approaches, the dog barks, and the intruder flees. The dog has become a trained guard dog, and will attempt to scare off anyone approaching the house. This problem is easily prevented by letting the dog get to know the postman before the barking becomes a habit. This can be done by taking the dog with you to meet the postman each day as he delivers the post. Try to get into a conversation with him, and even ask him if he will give the dog a tidbit or two. Most postmen and other callers at the house are willing to help. If the dog gets to know regular callers, such as the postman and the paper boy, before the guarding instinct is developed, he will accept them. However, a word of warning. Do not make the mistake of thinking that this problem, once developed, can be cured by allowing the dog to meet, and get to know, the postman. The dog will most probably bite because, to his way of thinking, the postman has ignored the verbal warning, and has not fled as he always has in the past, so the dog may take the warning a step further, and bite.

Another situation, where barking becomes a problem, is the dog who gets hysterical at the sound of the doorbell. Once again, the dog has been taught to react hysterically each time the bell rings. As often as not, the dog is lying quietly next to mum when the bell sounds. Mum and dad immediately jump up and react in, from the dog's point of view, a nervous and frightened way. Mum may attempt a quick tidy-up, and Dad may hurry to the door to save the visitors waiting. To the dog, this behaviour suggests danger, and he will react accordingly by barking. When the dog attempts to go with Dad to the door, he is grabbed by the collar and shouted at. Once again, the dog reacts to the actions of the other family members, as everything they do suggests danger. Within a short time, you have a dog that has been unintentionally trained to get hysterical at the sound of the doorbell. This problem is easily avoided if you take the time to sit for about ten to fifteen seconds after hearing the bell, then slowly stand up and stretch, before wandering off to answer the door. The dog will hear the bell, see little or no immediate reaction from the other family members, with no danger signals, and will never learn to react to the bell in the first place.

For the dog that has to be

Large, strong breeds, such as Newfoundlands, must never be allowed to lay down the law.

retrained, you must be willing to do a bit of work prior to reacting in the way described above. Choose an evening when you will be able to devote enough time to curing the dog of this problem. Attach two wires to the doorbell and another bell-push, leading back to your favourite armchair, where you can sit the rest of the evening watching television. Every couple of minutes press the bell, but ignore the dog's reaction completely. The first twenty or so times he will react as you have, unwittingly, taught him to do in the past. Do not reprimand him, or react in any way whatsoever. You may sound the bell more than a hundred times during the evening, but the dog will gradually stop reacting, and by the end of the evening he will be ignoring it completely. From then on, when visitors call, you should learn to react to the bell calmly, as described above, thereby removing the signals that excite the dog. The problem has been cured without the use of force or punishment.

AGGRESSION

Dogs who bite people, both strangers and family members, are becoming all too common. Generally a dog will bite for one of three reasons:

Dominant aggression, when the dog acts as the pack leader, either all of the time, or in certain situations.

Predatory aggression, when a dog is excited by fast-moving people or animals and the natural instinct to hunt, chase, and capture is awakened.

Fear aggression, which is usually seen in badly socialised, nervous animals.

Dominant Aggression

Many people who have problems with a dog who bites as a show of dominance refuse to believe that this is the cause of the problem, because most of the time the dog is a lovable, obedient pet. On closer investigation, it can be seen that the family members have signed a truce with the dog, and allow him, at certain times, to lay down the law. As long as the whole family sticks to the rules, the dog will not show aggression. Many a seemingly placid dog will growl if someone approaches his feed dish while he is eating, or will protect his bed, or a particular place in the house. Another will share a chair with the owner, if the owner is already sitting down when the dog decides to join him, but will growl if the roles are reversed and the owner attempts to join the dog, or remove him.

All growls are a warning, and often, if the warning is ignored or tolerated, the dog may go a step further, and bite. Usually aggression is a gradual thing, starting with a growl, going on to a snarl and showing teeth, and then developing into biting. Most dominance problems can be cured if the signs are recognised early on, and expert help is sought.

I have a somewhat controversial opinion on dominant aggression. I always ask the owners if they are frightened of the dog. If the answer is a definite "Yes", I advise

them to re-home the dog. Dominant aggression can be cured by an experienced person, using any of several methods and techniques available to avoid the situation that causes the aggression. However, a dog who has learnt that aggression causes fear in the owner not only thinks that he is the pack leader, but the owner thinks so too, and has, unintentionally, conveyed that message to the dog. Therefore, I advise removal of the dog, for the sake of safety. Obviously, I am talking about extreme cases, as many dogs are bluffing, and with expert guidance the problem can be easily resolved. If an owner is unwilling to re-home an aggressive dog, expert advice must be sought as soon as possible. Often an experienced person can give some guidelines on how to avoid conflict situations, even if the problem cannot be completely resolved.

Predatory Aggression
Typical examples of predatory aggression are dogs that chase sheep, cats, joggers, or even cars, or cyclists. The instinct to chase is

The adult dog's calm outlook on life is a direct result of early training.

inherent in all dogs, and a habit is often an inherent trait, coupled with opportunity. If the chance to chase moving objects, such as cats or rabbits, is suppressed in a young dog, the chances are that the adult dog will never attempt to chase, as he has been denied such opportunity in his youth. Puppies should be socialised with all other animals, and be taken to the park where there are cyclists and joggers, and taught to remain calm in their presence. In this way the dog will become used to such things and learn to accept them.

Once the problem has fully developed, the only real solution is to train the dog to such a level of obedience that you always have control over him, even at a distance. Failing this, you should avoid giving the dog the opportunity to chase, which often means keeping him on the lead at such times.

Fear Aggression

This aggression is most often seen in badly socialised dogs that do not willingly accept being handled or touched by people. Fear biters usually shy away when approached, and will try to avoid being touched. However, if such a dog is cornered, and feels trapped, he will often snap or even attack in, to his way of thinking, self-defence. Such dogs usually cower, with their ears back, and if these signals are ignored, will often bite. Usually, they behave normally with people they know. If you own such a dog, you should prevent strangers from attempting to pat him. If visitors are told to ignore the dog completely, and act as though he does not exist, he will sometimes come around. Even if he does not do so, he will not attack unless cornered, with no line of escape. Once the dog has reached maturity, trying to socialise him will have limited success, and many animal psychologists say that these dogs cannot be helped. Other forms of aggression include rage syndrome, seen in certain breeds, aggression towards other dogs, sexual aggression, and aggression cause by both mental and physical disorders. I strongly advise seeking expert help with all aggression problems because the problem is so potentially dangerous.

DESTRUCTIVENESS

Dogs that chew up furniture, clothing, children's toys, in fact almost anything, invariably do so when they are left at home alone.

However, it can also occur at night, or even if the dog is alone in one room while the rest of the family are watching television in another. There can be several reasons for this behaviour, including loneliness. Teething pain is often blamed, but usually this is not the cause, simply because of the type of objects that the dog chews. It can also be the result of playfulness. People often do not realise that dogs have to be taught to stay alone, that they are social creatures and need company. If a dog gradually gets used to being left alone, and the duration of his separation is slowly increased, destructiveness caused by separation anxiety can be avoided. Almost all destructiveness, for whatever reason, can be avoided by the use of an indoor kennel.

If a dog gets adequate exercise, attention, companionship and a correct upbringing and training, he will accept being alone for certain periods each day as a normal part of life. If playfulness is the cause of destructive acts, then, once again, an indoor kennel will resolve the problem. I believe that many canine behaviour therapists discount playfulness as a

Sensible training and socialisation can suppress natural aggression.

common cause of destructiveness, preferring to give the problem a far more imposing name such as 'separation anxiety' or 'displacement behaviour' which sounds far more interesting. Playing is a major part of a dog's life, and I believe that destructiveness is often caused by the dog playing. A puppy is often encouraged to play in the house, but as the dog matures, any attempt to play is corrected, and the dog is told to be quiet, or to go and lie down. The dog learns that playing when his owners are in the house is punished, but he can play to his heart's content if he is alone. This only becomes a problem when his choice of toy is wrong.

Some time ago I sat talking on the phone while my six-month-old puppy was running around the room. I forgot about him for a few moments, and when the phone call ended he ran up to me with a large piece of our fitted carpet in his mouth. He had decided to play with the carpet, and I did not see him to prevent him doing so. These things happen. However, when I told a colleague, also a dog trainer, about the incident, she immediately started to psychoanalyse the event, mentioning all possible suppressed anxieties that the dog could be suffering from. She found it difficult to accept that the dog was just playing and happened to choose a plaything that cost a few hundred pounds. She also overlooked the simple fact that if I had put the dog in his kennel while I was unable keep an eye on him, the problem would not have occurred.

In general, common sense, combined with good, consistent basic training, will result in a well-balanced dog with socially acceptable habits. Almost all problem dogs are the result of incorrect upbringing. Inexperienced dog owners will make mistakes, and one can expect problems from time to time. By trying to analyse the problem, and finding the cause, we can normally find the solution. Some problems that are age-related, such as house training, may disappear as the puppy gets older, whereas others, such as dominance and aggression, will only worsen as the dog matures. For these, specialist help should be sought before the problem becomes established. Whatever the problem, you do not have to accept it. This is unfair to both you and your dog.

7 Having Fun With Your Dog

It should now be obvious that I strongly advocate attending training classes with your puppy, and going on to basic obedience training classes, for at least the first year. At the end of this time you will have been given enough advice, and have gained enough knowledge, to understand the basic principles of coping with a dog, and your dog should be a well-behaved and social creature. Most probably, the classes were given by an instructor who has made a hobby, or profession, of dog training. You may have seen this person working his own dog, or you may have watched the more advanced classes in progress. Most of these people first attended classes for the same reason as you. They either needed advice with their new dog, or had problems that needed expert help, and were then bitten by the dog training bug. Dog training is an excellent hobby, and can give endless pleasure to both you and your dog. There are several recognised sports available today, and your local training club can advise which one is suitable for you.

In Competitive Obedience, dogs must carry out a series of set exercises and these are scored for accuracy and precision.

COMPETITIVE OBEDIENCE

This sport originated from basic pet dog training and consists, as the name implies, of training your dog to carry out different obedience exercises to an extremely high degree of accuracy. Competitions are held throughout the year, all over the country. There are seven classes to enter, and each dog starts at the lowest level, qualifying through the classes, towards the coveted title of Obedience Champion.

The first class that all new competitors enter is Pre-Beginners. This class is designed to introduce newcomers to the world of Competitive Obedience, and consists of the exercises Heel on lead, Heel free, Recall to Handler, Sit-stay, and Down-stay. Qualification to a higher class is achieved by winning a first place. Handler and dog must then progress through the classes; Beginners, Novice, Class A, Class B, and on to Class C. At special championship shows there is a further class, Championship Class C, eligible to dogs that have qualified to compete in this class. A dog or bitch who wins this class three times, under three different judges, gains the title of Obedience Champion. If a dog or bitch wins a championship class at a show he, or she, is eligible to compete in the Obedience Championships at Crufts Dog Show the following year.

Competitive Obedience is an extremely popular sport, and the larger competitions often have more than a thousand entries. More importantly, as with all canine sports, dog people are an extremely friendly group, with many attending just for the fun and enjoyment of a doggy day out with like-minded people.

AGILITY

This sport was developed in England in the 1970s, and has now spread throughout the world. Originally, Agility was started as a fun game, but has developed into a fully-fledged competitive sport. Agility consists of training a dog to jump, climb, run, and walk, over and under a variety of obstacles. This is done against the clock. Time penalties and points lost for incorrect work determine the winner. As with Obedience, this sport is open to both pedigree and non-pedigree dogs, although in most European countries only pedigree dogs are allowed to enter championship competitions. There are special classes for small breeds,

Agility is a fun sport for both dog and handler.

with the obstacles being altered to suit their stature. All that is needed to compete in Agility is average health and fitness, for both dog and handler.

Each Agility course is designed by the competition judge, and is different at each show. There are a minimum of ten, and a maximum of twenty, obstacles allowed, and the permitted obstacles are:
• hurdles and long jumps, which the dog must clear without fouling.
• a hoop or tyre, which the dog must jump through.
• a table which the dog must jump on to, and wait until commanded to leave.

• tunnels, both collapsible and rigid, through which the dog must run.
• weaving poles, that the dog must negotiate, alternating through each pole to the left and right.
• a ramp, consisting of two boards leaning together in an A-form, over which the dog must climb.
• a dog walk consisting of a plank between 10–12 inches wide, 12–14 feet long, and about 2 feet off the ground, over which the dog must walk (or run).
• a seesaw, similar to a child's seesaw over which the dog must walk.

Tackling the A-frame.

Emerging from the tunnel.

The sport of Mini-Agility means that the smaller breeds can also compete.

• a cross, over which is a cross-shaped platform which a dog must complete as directed by the handler.

Dogs love Agility work, and it is extremely rare to see a dog not working with great enthusiasm. The only drawback with Agility, as a hobby, is that so much specialist equipment is needed that the average dog owner can only train at a club, which may restrict training to once or twice a week.

FLYBALL

This sport originated in America and is gaining popularity throughout the world. It is a team knock-out competition, each team consisting of four dogs. Each dog must jump four hurdles, and run to an apparatus containing a tennis ball, which is released when the dog pushes a foot pedal with his front paws. The dog must then catch the ball and return, over the hurdles, to the handler, at which time the next dog is released. The team that retrieves all four tennis balls, without fault, in the quickest time, is the winner. As with Agility, this sport started off as a game and quickly developed into a competitive sport. Of all dog sports, it is probably the one with the greatest spectator attraction, and, as it is fairly simple to teach, it is attractive to pet dog owners who just want a bit of fun with their dogs.

WORKING TRIALS

Working Trials is the one sport that attracts both professionals, such as police dog-handlers, and pet owners. The sport consists of five sections: Control (obedience); Stays; Agility (jumps); Retrieve and nosework section (which includes searching and tracking); and the Patrol section which includes manwork (teaching a dog to pursue and hold a criminal).

Each dog must qualify through to a higher level. The titles awarded to qualifying dogs are: CD (companion dog), UD (utility dog), WD (working dog), TD (tracking dog) and PD (patrol dog). Manwork is included only in the PD qualification.

Obviously this is an outdoor sport, and the trials are often held over two days, which can be restrictive for the average dog owner due to the time involved

FIELD TRIALS

Field Trials are primarily intended to assess the ability, and quality of work, of Gundogs. Trials are divided into four sub-groups: Retrievers, Spaniels, Pointers and Setters, with a section for breeds

Working Trials attract professional handlers and pet owners.

that hunt, point, and retrieve. This sport may be of interest to owners of dogs belonging to the Gundog group. Many people are under the misapprehension that they have a moral obligation to train their dogs for this type of activity, simply because their dog is classed as a gundog, and they believe that, if they fail to do so, their dog will be unfulfilled. This, of course, is nonsense. A house pet will be perfectly happy without the activity for which his ancestors were originally bred. The only reason to enter Field Trials or to train your dog for this sport is because you want to.

JUST HAVING FUN

Apart from the organised sports mentioned above, it is possible to invent lots of pastimes and games to entertain your dog, and keep him mentally alert, without all the time-consuming effort needed for competition work. My dogs are Frisbee-mad, and are taken out for a game at least once a day. Throwing a ball or toy during the daily walk is just as much fun, but do not get into the habit of throwing sticks for your dog. I have lost count of the number of dogs who have injured themselves by rushing off to retrieve a stick which they have grabbed end on, with the result that the stick has

Field Trials are designed to assess the working ability of the gundog breeds.

walk. Of course, some dogs are better at seeking than others, so remember to count the kids before starting off for home! This game can be adapted for indoors during wet weather, with the kids hiding under the bed, or in cupboards. It is also a good game for grown-ups, although you may not want to admit that to your friends.

Dogs love to use their noses, and it is very simple to develop this trait into a game. Play with the dog using a ball, or some other toy, and then restrain him by the collar while you throw the ball into some long grass a few feet away. Tell the dog to find, and send him to get the ball. Gradually you can build up the distance until he will search quite a large area. A variation on this is to walk across a field and take the dog by the collar, then turn around and let him see that you are dropping his ball. Lead him off a few yards, and then turn him around and tell him to "Find it". As he gains confidence, the distance can be increased. At first the dog will be able to see the ball, but as you get further away he will no longer be able to see it, and will start to use his nose. Dogs can easily seek-back for a mile or more, and learn to do this quite quickly. The dog

The family dog will enjoy helping with tasks around the home.

gone down their throat.

Another great game for the kids, as well as the dog, is hide and seek. Hold the dog, and send the kids to hide, then send the dog off after them. Until the dog understands what is required, the children will have to call him a few times, but he will soon get the idea. The whole family can take part, and endless hours can be spent with this game during a can be taught to search the house for his toy. Just place the toy, half hidden behind a chair leg, or under the sofa, and tell the dog to "Find it". As he does so, encourage him with lots of praise to bring it back to you, and then hide it somewhere else, each time making it slightly more difficult to find. As the dog gains experience, the toy can be hidden in quite

difficult places, and he will be able to find it by using his nose with apparent ease.

All these games, and there are lots that you can invent with a little imagination, help to keep the dog mentally active, and prevent boredom by giving him something to do. They also help to establish a better relationship between you and your dog.

Training does not always have to be serious – these dogs enjoy the stimulation of learning a new exercise.

A–Z of Dog Diseases & Health Problems

288 pages
150 colour illustrations

Price £14.99

The definitive work on health care. Written by Guide Dogs for the Blind veterinary consultant Dick Lane and breeding manager Neil Ewart

Competitive Obedience For Winners

143 pages
58 b&w illustrations

Price £15.99

Brian McGovern's highly acclaimed book for those who want to take dog training a step further.

New edition Doglopaedia

264 pages

Price £8.95

The outstanding work on general dog care, including health and behavioural problems. Written by veterinary surgeon Jim Evans and Kay White.